CW00521882

Be More Snail

FIND JOY AND THRIVE BY LIVING IN THE SLOW LANE

Be More Snail

POP PRESS

**FIND JOY
AND THRIVE
BY LIVING
IN THE
SLOW LANE**

The Way of the Snail

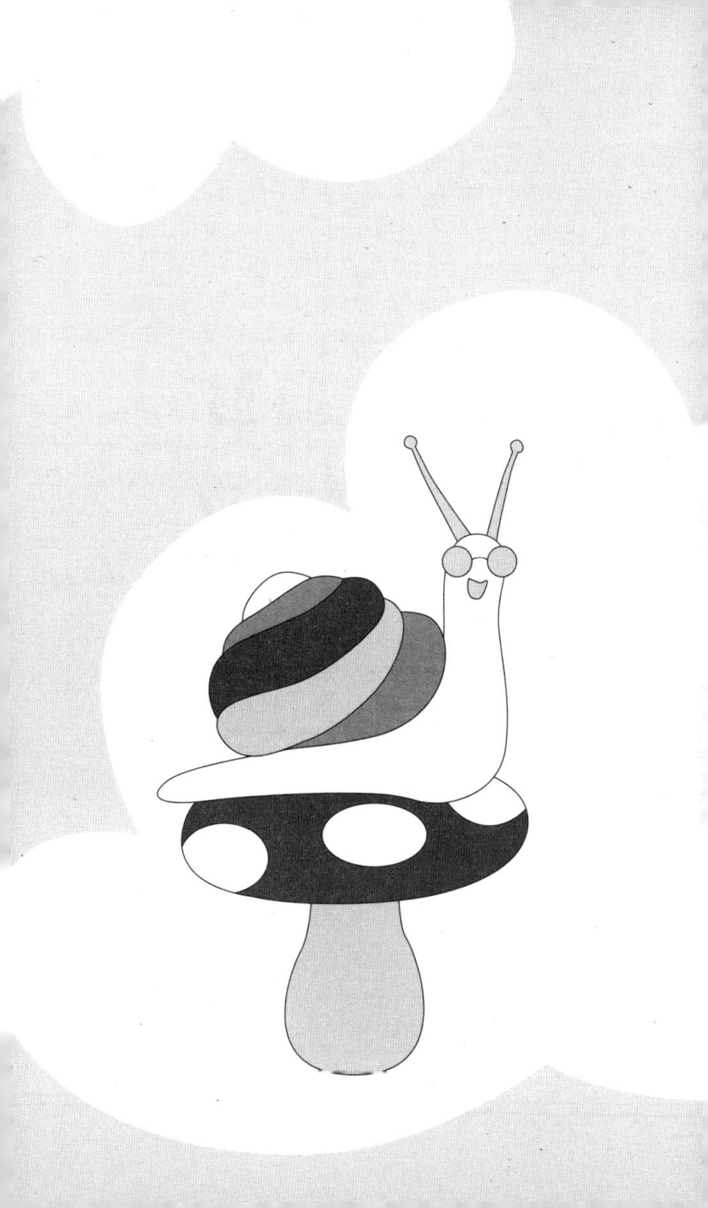

If your life is racing by in a crazy blur of WhatsApp messages, Insta posts, work emails and mindless junk TV, it might be time to look to our plant-loving neighbour for help.

When everything feels a bit too much, the humble snail can show us how to put the brakes on and embrace life in the slow lane. Following a more sedate lifestyle gives you time to think and breathe; you will find you have more space to make good decisions and choices that work for you. With help from our snail friends, the benefits of the slow lane don't have to be a distant dream, and once we master the art of slowing down, we will quickly see just

4 how fulfilled and meaningful our lives can be.

The snail carries its home on its back and knows when to retreat into it for some quiet downtime. It's a creature that knows what it likes – usually a quiet, shady and leafy place of peace – and it is smart enough to stay away from what's not good for it, including harsh sunlight, saltiness and places where unexpected things can pounce. In other words, the snail can teach us a lot about protecting our vulnerabilities without needing to build walls so high that nobody can scale them to reach us. By learning from the snail, we begin to understand when it's right for us to come out and shine and when we should retreat and embrace introvert life.

The snail knows how to look after itself, too. Its shell is beautiful and unique, and the mucus it produces to help it to glide along in life keeps its skin healthy and has amazing moisturising properties – so the snail knows the importance of a great self-care routine!

This book is divided into the nine core lessons that we can learn from the humble snail. You can dip in and out and read the sections in any order you please, the most important thing is to take your time and let the steady wisdom of our plant-loving neighbour sink in. Grab a nice cup of tea, or whatever you fancy. A gentle and fulfilled life is just a few leisurely chapters away.

In *Slow Down* we'll discover all the joys and benefits of taking life at a slower pace. The snail takes its home everywhere it goes, so in *Your Body is Your Home* we'll learn to how to love and care for our own snail homes – our bodies. *Eat More Plants* has lots of tips about sneaking more healthy plant-based dishes into your diet, and in *Don't Be Salty* we'll discover the things we need to avoid if we truly want to be more snail and happier.

Snails like to roam, so *Explore Green Spaces* encourages us to get outdoors and connect with the healing power of nature and in *Perseverance is Key* we see how the humble snail teaches us that success is not just about hard work, it is about staying power and never, ever giving up.

In the last part of the book, we embrace all the things that make the snail unique.

6   *Embrace What Makes You Different* celebrates diversity and teaches us to revere what makes us stand out from the crowd, and in *Love Your Small-space Sanctuary,* you will see how less really is more. Finally, in *Retreat and Embrace Introvert Life* you'll discover how choosing to spend time alone can be not only energising but the highest form of self-care.

Once you start to notice the snail and learn the life lessons it can share, you're on your way to forging your own unique snail trail through life. You'll learn how to appreciate the little things, take pleasure in the moment, destress and glide serenely through all the adventures that life throws at you.

Slow Down

Down

**(and appreciate
the little things)**

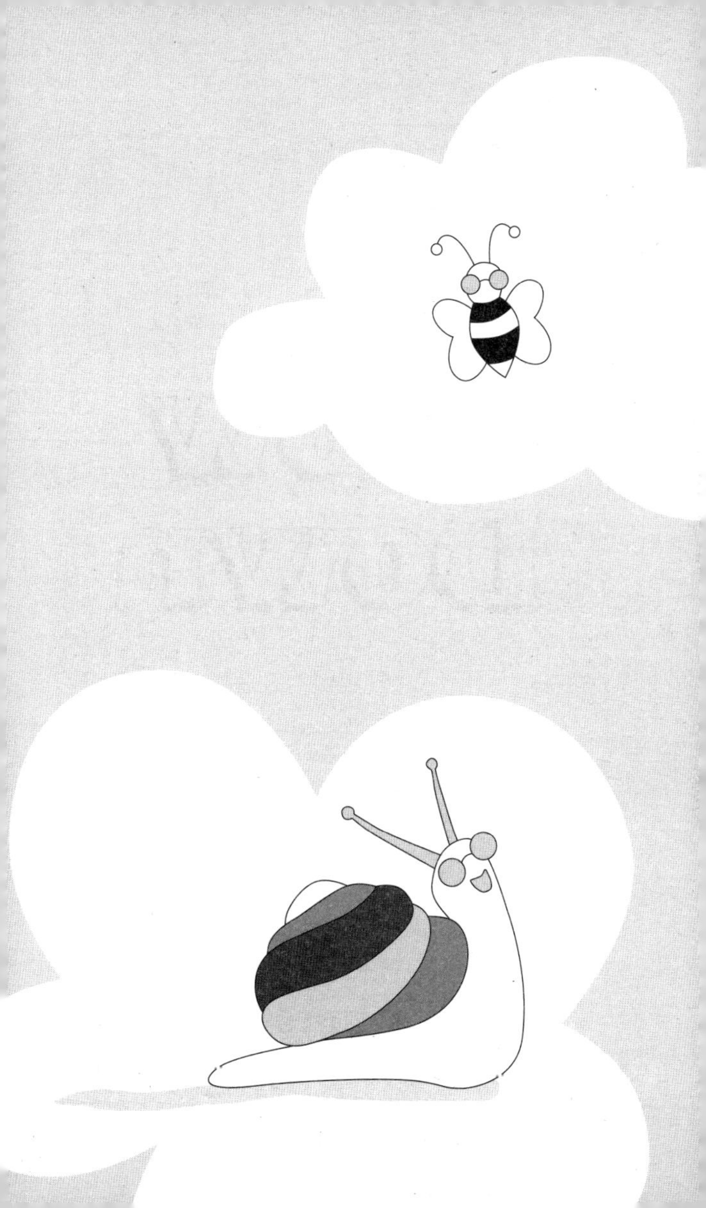

Modern life is complex. More and more of us find ourselves committed to busy routines, the constant demand of messages and stressful workloads that have us wishing the weeks away and living just for the weekends when we can switch off.

It doesn't have to be this way. A slow-paced life doesn't mean a boring one and taking time out for a short while every day of the week can really help to establish what it is that you need to truly thrive. Taking the lead from our snail friends means carving out time to enjoy whatever we're doing; it means single-tasking,

12   disconnecting from apps and tech, giving
yourself the mental space to breathe and
being present in the moment.

When we adopt a snail-inspired Slow
Living lifestyle we become more present
and more willing to walk away from that
which no longer serves us.

We learn how to do what's important
and we forget what doesn't matter.

We end up, as a result of slowing down,
feeling more grounded and more free
because we've taken back control of our
time, our attention and our lives.

Here are a few easy steps to help you to slow down in your life:

1.

Disconnect. Switch off and switch 'it' off. 'It' might be your mobile, your laptop, your iPad or your TV. Whatever technology you use, take regular breaks from it so that you can give your overwrought mind some well-deserved respite from information overload.

It can be hard to take the first step in disconnecting, so start simple. Try switching off for that last hour of the evening before you go to bed. If you can, leave your phone to charge somewhere other than in the bedroom. If you use it as an alarm and you're worried about over-sleeping, get yourself an old-fashioned alarm clock instead.

If you want to check your favourite Insta account or post to your own, set a timer to limit yourself to no longer than 30 minutes. Or commit to only checking social media once a day, with a time limit on your scrolling.

Once you get into these new habits you can step up to a longer social media detox. Deactivate your accounts for a day, a weekend – or even a whole week – and focus instead on the world around you!

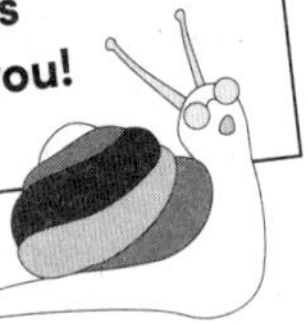

2.

Be present. It takes practice to stay in the present and not allow the mind to flit between the past and the future or be distracted by a busy to-do list.

To get started, block out time in your day to sit and do something quiet, like have a cup of tea, and really focus on what's going on in that moment. What can you see around you? What can you hear? What can you smell?

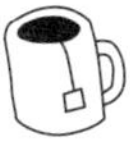

3.

Breathe. Checking in with your breath is a fast-track way to slow your mind and flood the brain with a feel-good, calming neurotransmitter (natural chemical messenger) called noradrenaline. The more you slow down, the more acute your ability to focus and pay attention becomes. Noradrenaline is released when we are curious, challenged or emotionally aroused. It can help the brain form new neural pathways and is sometimes called a brain 'fertiliser'.

So, find a breathing practice that suits you and see for yourself how slowing the breath sharpens the mind and helps you with problem solving and stress busting.

Build your breath practice into your daily routine. Do it before breakfast, on your commute, or anywhere you can safely practise for a few minutes.

4.

Join the Slow Food revolution. Slow right down in the kitchen and take time to prepare your food. Designate days of the week when you cook from scratch and avoid reaching for fast food or takeaways. Take your time through the whole process – from choosing a recipe to preparing your ingredients, and then cooking the dish.

Use a print cookbook – if you don't have any, head to the charity shop or the local library and find a preloved one. Flicking through the pages will focus you on the task in hand and keep you off your smartphone.

Turn the art of meal preparation into a slow food ritual; inhale and enjoy the scent of any herbs and spices you are using. Chop every vegetable with a sense of gratitude towards those who sowed the seeds, who nurtured and harvested the plant and played any role in its journey from the soil to your plate.

Snail Fact

The snail is so appreciative of its preferred foods it will even sleep beside a favourite mushroom or leaf. You don't need to sleep beside your finished dish, but you might like to take your new cookbook to bed for some soothing bedtime reading.

Snail Fact

It would take a garden snail five days and 12 hours to move just one mile.

Your Body is Your Home

(treat it with kindness)

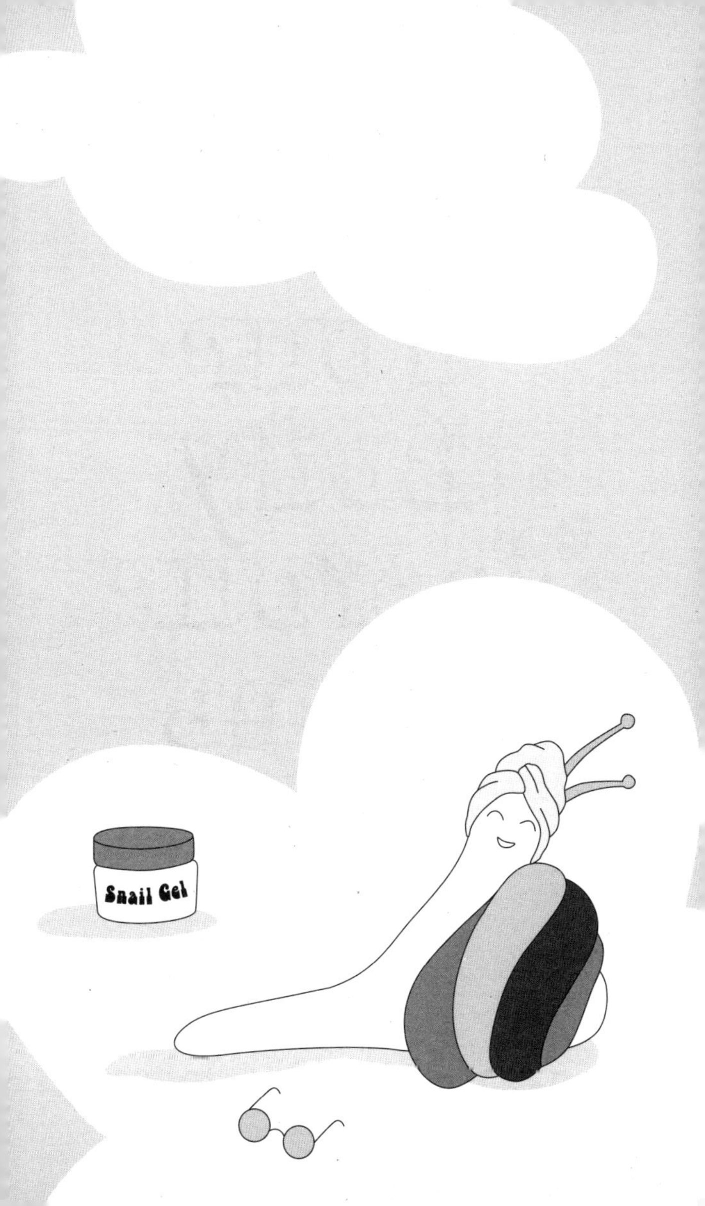
Snail Gel

You may think that when it comes to taking care of your home that you and the snail have nothing in common – because you leave yours behind when you step out of the front door whereas the snail takes theirs with them everywhere. But the home you're thinking about is bricks and mortar and you're forgetting about the true home that you carry with you every day.

Your true 'home' is – just as it is for the snail – your body, which houses everything that makes up you, both physically and mentally – muscles, bones, blood vessels, nerves, emotions, thoughts and more.

24 A snail's shell is made from calcium carbonate, along with small amounts of protein, and is made by the mantle – a sac-like structure in the body wall that emits an electrical pulse to push calcium ions into place to form a hard shell. Snails are physically attached to their shells and cannot survive without them. They can make small repairs to dents and damage, but they will die if they are torn from their private and protective little fortresses, needing that safe space, just as we do.

The key life lesson that the snail offers us when we think about our body as our home is one that reveals the importance of self-care. This means treating our bodies with kindness and respect, prioritising taking time out from our busy lives to repair dents and damage, allowing ourselves space to grow and recognising the importance of staying strong and keeping mobile.

Try these tips on how to treat your body with kindness:

1.

Leave space to grow. As the snail grows, so does its shell, and as you moved from childhood to adulthood, you got bigger too. But the idea of growth is not limited to the physical body, and when people talk about 'growing as a person' they mean in terms of maturity, wisdom and understanding. Growth like this does not happen without work and that work usually comes in the form of life experience and/or study to make sense of the world we live in and what happens to us.

If you want to be more snail, make time for an activity that will help you to grow stronger in body, mind and spirit. This could be a regular yoga practice or even something like running or swimming, which for many can become more like a meditation and so benefit your mind as well as your physical body.

2.

Get a grip. The snail can only move forward by keeping a firm grip on what's real – which is the ground under its large foot! Copy the snail; get a grip on those things that can affect your body and its functioning, stay grounded, take time out for yourself and don't let the demands of others overwhelm you.

Think: are you doing everything you can to nourish and nurture your 'home'? Are you eating properly, sleeping well and making healthy lifestyle choices, or do you need to think about making some changes that will better support a healthy 'home'?

If you are feeling run down, stop and take a self-care day. Bake a cake, put on a face mask, read a book in a long hot bath. Build self-care practices into your schedule to give yourself some quiet time and allow your body and mind to recover.

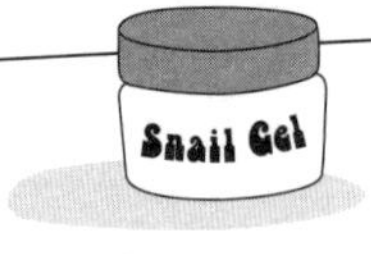
Snail Gel

3.

Trust your body. The snail knows how to trust its powerful sense of smell to find food and will also react to any sense of danger by retreating into its shell. In other words, it trusts its body and the messages it sends to its brain, which is something we can all learn to do better, too.

Have you heard of Interoception? It's one of the fastest-moving areas of neuroscience and psychology. Scientists are exploring how the internal systems of the body communicate with each other, and they have discovered that we can learn to 'tune in' to these messages and that when we do so, we can enhance our wellbeing and wellness.

Although a lot of this internal communication is below conscious awareness, scientists now believe there are signals and sensations such as heartbeat and breath patterns that we can learn to 'read' and react to. For example, if you saw a snarling dog your stomach would tighten, your heart rate would increase, but you'd know you're feeling anxious and stressed and so would be better able to regulate these sensations of fear.

Scientists also now believe the process of interoception – which is still in its infancy as a field of research – lies behind our intuition and that sense we get of an inner knowing when something is right or wrong, even when we cannot explain why.

When, like the snail, we trust our intuition we can learn to make good choices for our physical and emotional wellbeing and keep our bodies safe and our 'home' running smoothly. So get into the habit of checking in with yourself and your body each morning. Do a mental scan from top to toe and try to notice the signals your body is sending the brain. Is your breath calm and your heartrate steady? Do you feel good or is there any underlying anxiety niggling away? The more you practise this the better you'll get at 'reading' yourself and regulating your emotions.

4.

Stretch yourself. They say use it or lose it, and stretching is a great way to keep your 'home' flexible and up to the task of providing your forever base. Try to spend at least 10 minutes a day stretching, especially your spine.

Here's a simple exercise that you can, as you become more snail, expand on and practise daily. Your body will love and thank you for making time to do this energising good-morning stretch.

- ✿ Stand with your feet hip-width apart and raise your arms right up over your head.
- ✿ Keep the arms straight and feel the muscles at the top of the back working hard to lift them and keep them raised.
- ✿ Keep your focus on the palms of your hands, which should be facing each other. You may start to feel some heat being generated between them.

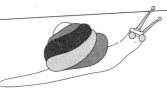

Your Body is Your Home

* Now take your gaze upwards to look at your hands and feel the delicious stretch at the front of your throat.

* Hold this position and try to feel a long stretch right up through your body, and when you think you can't stretch another inch, reach up a little higher.

Snail Fact

Just like people, snails of the same variety share common characteristics, but their shells can vary in size and colour between individual creatures. This, as with hair or eye colour in people, is a result of their genetic inheritance.

Eat More Plants

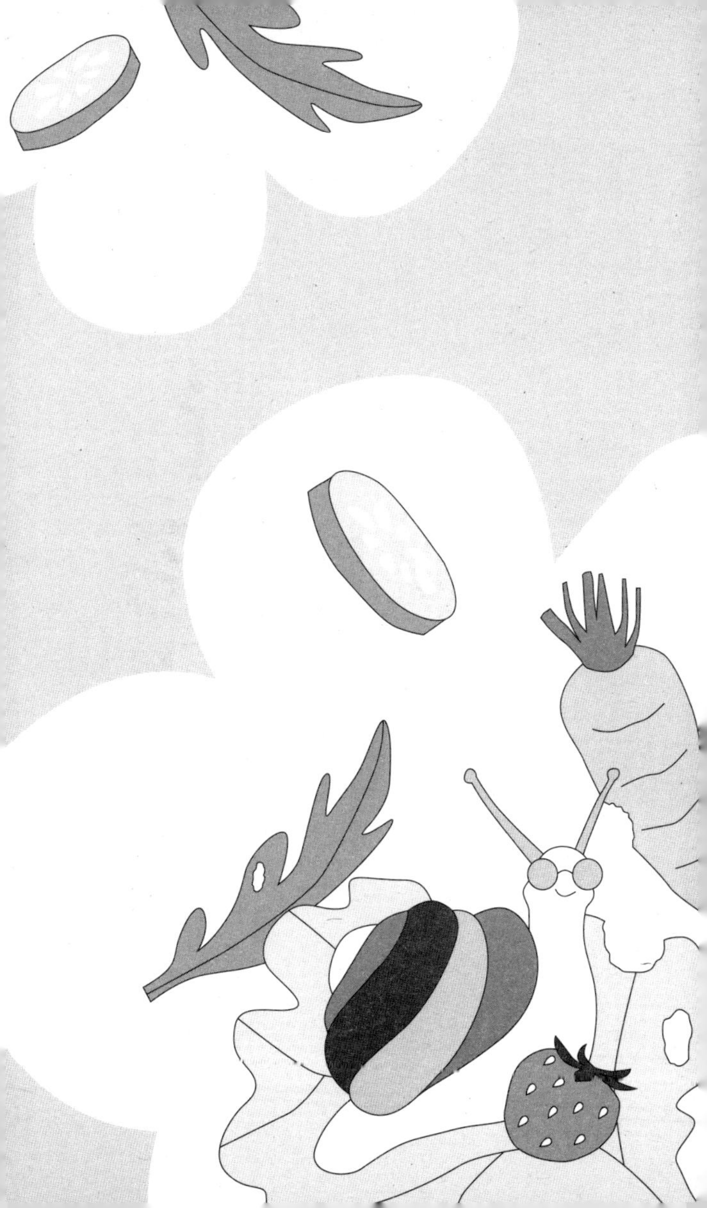

Whilst snails have evolved to eat just about anything – including decaying waste from other animals and plants – there's no question that what land snails like best is a crunchy vegetable, especially in the shape of a cucumber, a tender broccoli stem, a curly lettuce or a juicy cabbage leaf.

When it comes to food choices, though, snails set us an excellent example of zero-waste living, because they eat every part of the plant – the stems, leaves, bark, flowers and fruits.

A snail will hunt for food using its extraordinarily powerful sense of smell and will often build fat stores when food is plentiful so they can survive the winter by hibernating when food sources are scarce.

Even more extraordinary, a snail can voluntarily put its own body into a state of aestivation – or dormancy – in order to survive severe drought conditions.

We can learn from the snail how to feed our bodies in line with the seasons, and to feed them what they need, when they need it. By choosing a way of eating that generates less water and in line with what nature is producing, we can look after ourselves as well as our planet.

Here's how you can be more snail in what you eat and at the same time protect our precious planet:

1.

Throw less away. You can copy the snail and adopt a 'Less-waste' policy in your own kitchen with your veggies. Lots of us habitually discard the roots or tops of leeks and spring onions, but don't chuck them out, instead roast them whole and eat them in a rolled pancake with a soy dipping sauce. You can even regrow the ends of sweet potatoes by allowing them to root in a glass of water, then pot them on.

Or how about making a delicious carrot salsa with the tops you would normally throw away? To make the carrot-top salsa, blitz the feathery green carrot tops with a couple of cloves of garlic, a cup of olive oil, a quarter of a cup of red wine vinegar, the zest and juice of a lemon, two jalapeno peppers (diced) and a generous pinch of dried oregano.

2.

Do your bit to protect the climate with a plant-based diet. Switching to a plant-based diet like our friend the snail is one of the easiest ways to reduce your environmental impact on the planet. The positives of this change can be even more impactful than cutting down on aeroplane flights or driving an electric car, because whilst these actions help reduce carbon emissions, they don't tackle the problem of the industrial-scale farming of animals, which is hugely detrimental to the environment and the planet's resources.

If a complete switch to being plant-based is too daunting, take a half-way step and try eating no meat for a week, or introducing plant-based days.

Easy veggie swaps include switching diced mushrooms for minced meat to make lasagne or Bolognese sauce, scrambling tofu spiced with turmeric as an alternative to scrambled eggs, and serving veggie kebabs with braised fennel and roasted tomatoes instead of chicken, lamb or beef.

3.

Value and protect your resources. The snail has learned to value its resources and can even put itself into a state of near dormancy to survive food and water shortages. This teaches us to become more aware of our own 'resources', which can include food but also money, work, love, support and even our health.

The snail would never squander what it needs to survive, and neither should we.

Make a list of the resources you know are available to you right now. This can include your job, support from loving family and friends, your ability to feed and nurture yourself and to find love and to cherish it when you do.

Now think about the resources that may be lacking in your life. Perhaps love is proving elusive or work is not guaranteed?

The snail teaches us there is always a solution to the challenges that come our way, so list how you can seek out and sustain the resources you need. If you would like a romantic partner, how can you find someone who will share the same values as you? If you need more meaningful work, think about your existing networks and who might be able to help you find a new and more fulfilling role.

Ask for help where you need it. Family, friends and work colleagues can all provide important resources and support.

4.

Sniff out great opportunities. The snail uses its sense of smell to find its food. You could say it spends much of its time sniffing out breakfast, lunch and dinner. We can learn from the snail to follow our noses to find the things in life that help us to be the best version of ourselves that we can be.

Sometimes, what's best for us is not what we want but what we need, and often these are the golden opportunities that come to us from unexpected places. For example, you may decide to volunteer at a local charity shop as part of your new slower-paced lifestyle and in meeting a new social and work circle, you might be offered a change of direction in your career that allows you to finally use all your skills.

The golden rule in sniffing out great opportunities is to keep your nose to the ground and dig deep to uncover more meaning and fulfilment in your life.

Snail Fact

The average garden snail has around 14,000 microscopic teeth which are called radula, and which the snail uses not to bite or chomp through its food but to 'scrape' it.

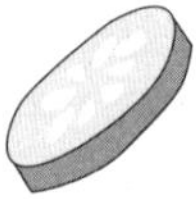

Don't Be Salty

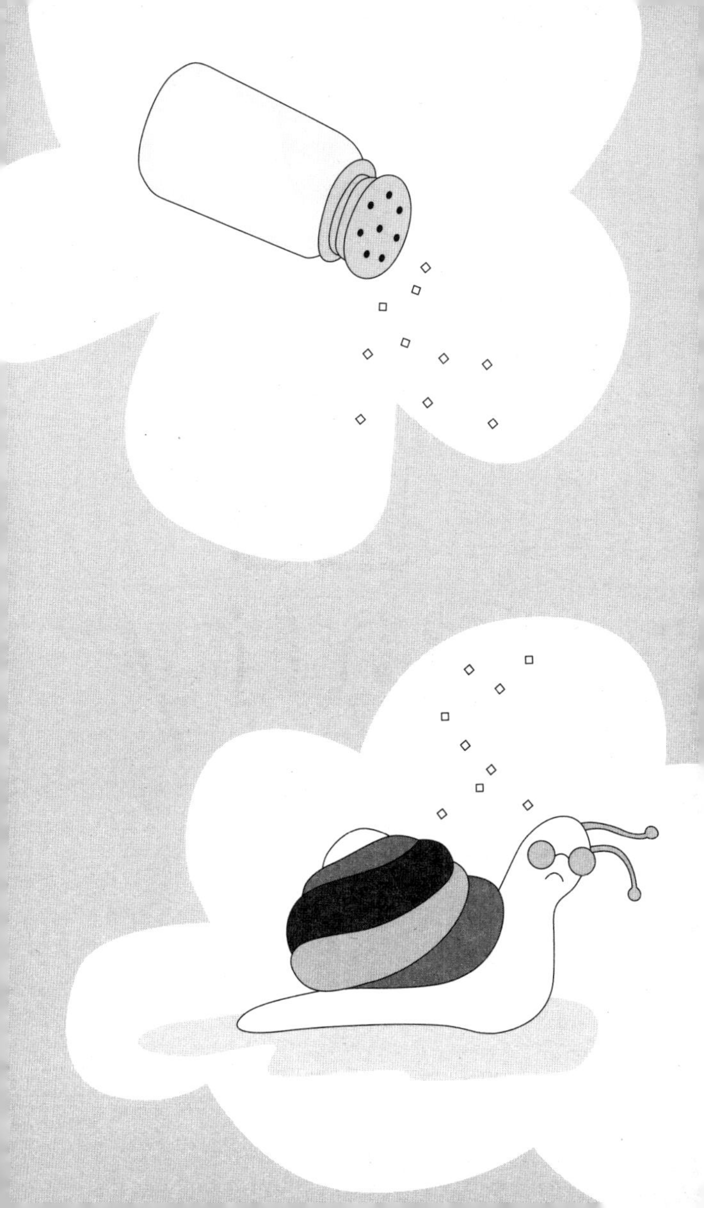

Snails have very good reason to avoid salt. If they come into contact with it it draws all the moisture from their bodies. It dehydrates and hurts them, and being salty can hurt us as well as others.

If you find yourself often saying or thinking negative things about someone, obsessing over the success of other people in comparison to your own successes, it might be time to try the snail way and avoid saltiness at all costs. It's a hard thing to do when we are bombarded every day with the perfect images that people post on social media, but in time you can learn to change your perception and stop what psychologists call 'upward comparisons'.

48 Upward comparisons are when we compare ourselves to anyone that we feel is better looking than us, has a better career, seems happier and appears to take for granted all the things that we yearn for. Comparing ourselves in this way can lead to jealousy and we may even find ourselves saying or doing mean things that not only hurt the person we think we envy but that also hurt us. In the same way that a snail will dry up on contact with salt, when we're salty about others, our self-esteem shrivels too.

But if we take a lesson from the wisdom of snails, we will go out of our way to avoid being salty and also learn how to better process the hurts when other people are jealous and 'salty' towards us.

Try these techniques to prevent yourself succumbing to upward comparisons and to instead appreciate the success in your own life.

49

1.

Manifest positive goals. You can't just avoid negative thoughts and feelings altogether – nobody can. But you can learn some simple techniques that will help you to work through these feelings, allowing them to pass through your mind and off into the ether.

If you see someone who appears to have everything you don't yet have in your life, stop and think about the two most important words in this sentence: 'appears' and 'yet'. Everybody likes to present their best selves in public, and with all the filters and photoshop options now available, that's never been easier to do. But we all know that many of those gorgeous selfies have been tweaked! So what you see is not what you would meet, face-to-face. In other words, nothing is as it appears and what you feel envious of may not even be real.

Now let's think about the word 'yet'. You may see a friend planning their wedding or a work colleague off on the trip of a lifetime and feel a terrible stab of jealousy. That's the salt hitting your eye! How about, instead of feeling jealous, you remind yourself that all things are possible, and if these wonderful things can happen for other people they can also happen for you. You are every bit as deserving; all you need to do is keep believing it will be your turn soon too. We can't eliminate jealousy – our own or other people's – but we can notice where it shows up and see this as being given information about what we really want in our own lives and perhaps even how we can get it.

To help focus on the good things heading your way, why not make a Pinterest board showcasing everything you hope will happen in your life? This can relate to your personal life, your relationships, your work and your fun activities. Find images of others who are already doing what you hope to do in your life and post these on your own 'inspo boards' to keep yourself believing.

2.

Make a book of gratitude. A gratitude book can be a lasting reference to everything we already have in our lives that makes us feel happy, hopeful and grateful for the little things. Your book has an important and ongoing job to do because you can reach for it every time you start to feel yourself in the grip of a downward spiral that is making it hard to hang on to your self-esteem.

Once you have reminded yourself that you already have much to be grateful for and even more to hope for, change your energy by going for a walk, taking a long hot bath or offering to do something nice for someone. Again, we can't just decide we'll never have a 'salty' negative thought again, but we can learn how to invite other, more positive ideas to the forefront of our minds and this very act will encourage those negative notions to leave us.

And remember that for those who might have had a scary brush with sickness or survived an accident, just being able to walk/talk/work and live independently will be reasons to be grateful – all the things that many of us just take for granted!

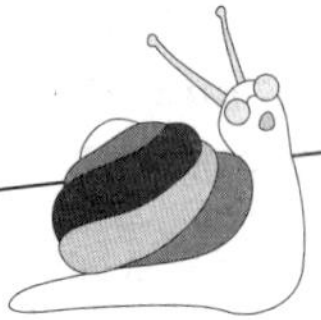

3.

Toxic positivity. It's true that positive people give off positive vibes and can often seem to attract good things, but there's a hidden depth to people who learn from salty challenges and work out how to dig a little deeper to navigate through them.

It's not as simple as saying just turn those negative thoughts into positive ones, it's more a case of accepting the negative feelings, allowing them to pass and, as you do so, finding things to feel more positive about. Anyone who suffers from any form of depression will tell you that you don't improve by burying the emotions or pretending you don't feel sad and hopeless, you recover by learning how to process those feelings so that you can live alongside them. For most people that means asking for help.

Yes, you can be your own counsellor, but you will get much further much faster along the road to recovery with the guidance of a professional therapist, so if you are feeling depressed, don't try to navigate it alone, get help!

4.

Stop hate-following. Hate-following is when you decide to follow someone on social media even though you know that you disagree with their views or actions, or you just don't like them. Research suggests that people do this as a source of entertainment, because they can get a sense of enjoyment from the adrenaline that comes from the 'how dare they!' moment. It can also help to diffuse pent-up emotions when we share pictures or posts from people that we don't like with people who feel the same way as us about them. But in fact all it does is keep us in a negative mindset. While it's important to expose ourselves to new ways of thinking, and to learn from them, if you find yourself expending energy in this way you should assess what's right for you. Are you learning from this process? Or are you just recycling anger? If it's the latter, perhaps it's time to unfollow the accounts that make you feel this way and commit to a more positive social media experience.

Snail Fact

Snails dehydrate after coming into contact with salt, so they can no longer create a snail trail to escape. Once immobilised, the snail becomes a sitting duck for anything that sees them as a tasty snack.

Explore Green Spaces

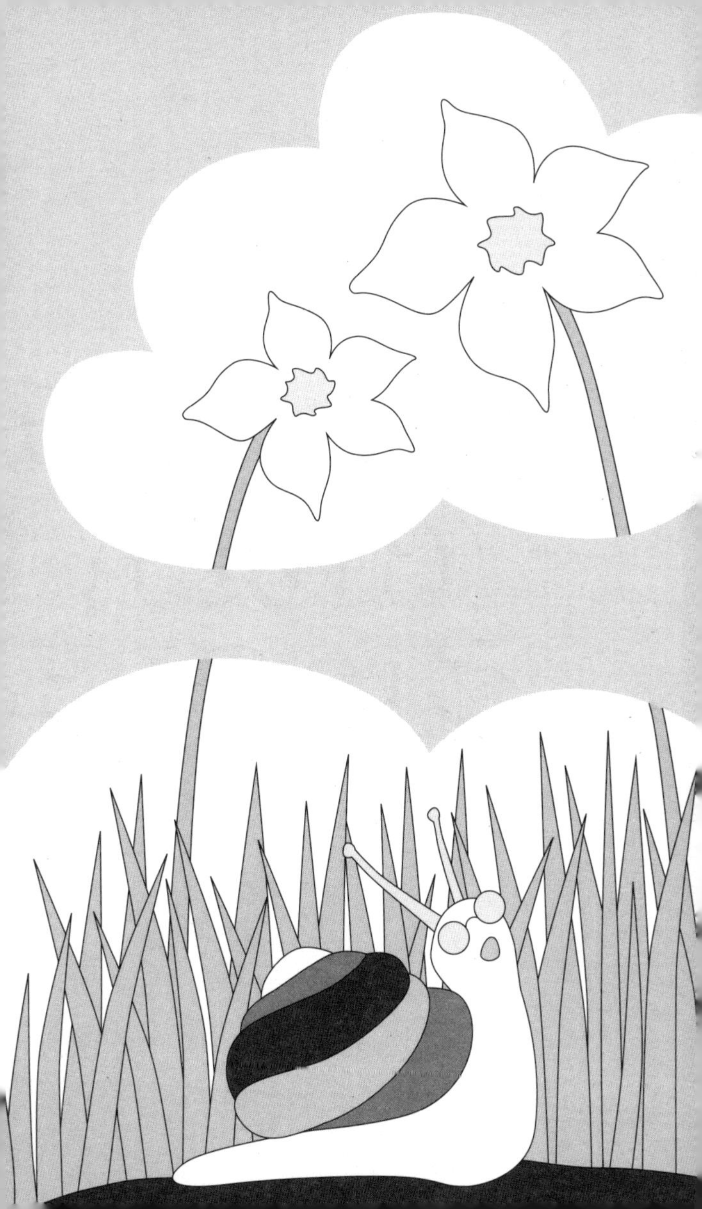

Snails have two dark-coloured eyes which can sense, rather than see, light and dark. This perception enables them to hide away from would-be predators, taking refuge in dark places like rocks, leaves and logs if they need to. And if you know you can easily hide or retreat (which is what snails do all day until it is safe to come out at night), then you can be braver about exploring open spaces and new terrain – especially green ones.

This is a lesson we can all learn from the snail.

It can be advantageous to be more adventurous; for the snail, exploring new terrain can mean finding a new food supply; for us, exploring new green spaces can mean feeling more deeply connected to the natural world and enjoying all the benefits that come with those feelings. But it is always wise to do this in a way, like the snail, that keeps us safe. For example, you would not set off on a mountain trek in a remote location without a guide, a map and a compass.

If we spend a lot of time indoors and online, we can actively choose to get outside and use nature and the outdoor world – which is the snail's natural environment – to help us become the best version of ourselves that we can be and to keep our brains and our bodies healthy.

Most of us spend much of our day multi-tasking and bombarding the prefrontal cortex of the brain, which then has to process all this information. Getting outdoors and into green spaces not only gives this part of the brain a well-deserved rest but allows all those other parts that are concerned with creative thinking, problem-solving and just feeling good about life and ourselves to take over for a while.

So let's be more snail and embrace our natural world. Here are a few ways to explore the green spaces around us.

1.

Even just looking at a green space can make us feel less stressed. Walking in nature has been proven to reduce anxiety and stress. When, as part of a controlled experiment, Japanese researchers compared the heart rate and blood pressure of those walking in a forest to those walking in the city, they found the forest walkers had lower heart rates, lower blood pressure and reported less stress and being in a better mood than those in the city.

If you can't get outside, even just looking out of the window at greenery can soothe feelings of stress and anxiety, so if you work from home and have this option, try to put your desk somewhere with a lovely view.

2.

Immersing ourselves in green spaces makes us more positive. Leave your smartphone in your rucksack and go for a long walk somewhere beautiful, such as a park, an arboretum or along a coastal path.

As you walk, think about the things that might be troubling you or are proving a challenge to resolve. Are there any upsets at work or at home that are keeping you awake at night? Are you struggling to find a way through the issues?

Trust that this walk will help you come up with the answers you need because scientists who have studied our problem-solving abilities have discovered that hiking in nature helps people to focus more creatively and successfully on problem-solving – but only if they put their phones away.

3.

Green spaces make us kinder and more generous. Researchers at the University of California, Berkeley, set up an experiment to see if exploring green spaces helps to make people more generous, trusting and willing to help others – and they found the answer was a resounding: yes!

They came up with a game that measured generosity and trust and discovered that those participating were kinder when they were shown beautiful landscapes and scenery than those who were shown less-green images. The scientists concluded that even surrounding participants with beautiful green plants made them feel more positive about life and left them more disposed to helping others.

We can easily recreate these positive vibes in our homes by growing and nurturing houseplants that will make us feel happy when we look at them, and kind when we take the trouble to care for them.

And if a houseplant can make you feel that good, imagine all the positive emotions that will flood your brain when you place yourself outdoors in a beautiful landscape or any natural and healing environment.

4.

Find life and joy in nature. Being outdoors and exploring green spaces will make you feel more alive and engaged with the world.

Understanding the importance of unplugging from the virtual worlds that demand so much of your time and stepping out into the real, natural world will make you feel better, think better, understand others better and like yourself better. It might make you want to share the message, too. You can help to conserve the environment by volunteering for a charity that promotes the benefits of nature, or one that preserves the natural habitat of endangered species.

5.

Get more green around you. The colour green is often used to symbolise rebirth, renewal and regeneration. In other words, it is the colour of hope. Green also has a profound psychological impact on the brain and is said to encourage a balance that leads to decisive thinking and problem-solving.

If you need a mental boost or help solving a problem, take five minutes from your day to sit and contemplate the colour green. You can focus on the green leaf of a plant, a green cushion or a green football field. Even better, go outside and pick a blade of newly sprouted grass, if you can find one.

Now, sit back and let green do its thing. Allow a sense of clarity and peace to enfold you, and know that whenever you are feeling anxious or stressed, all you need to do is find something green to sit with for a while.

Snail Fact

Snails have an extraordinary homing instinct, and according to university scientists who studied the distances that snails can travel – and still find their way home – you'd have to take a snail at least 20 metres from your garden to prevent it coming back.

Perseverance is Key

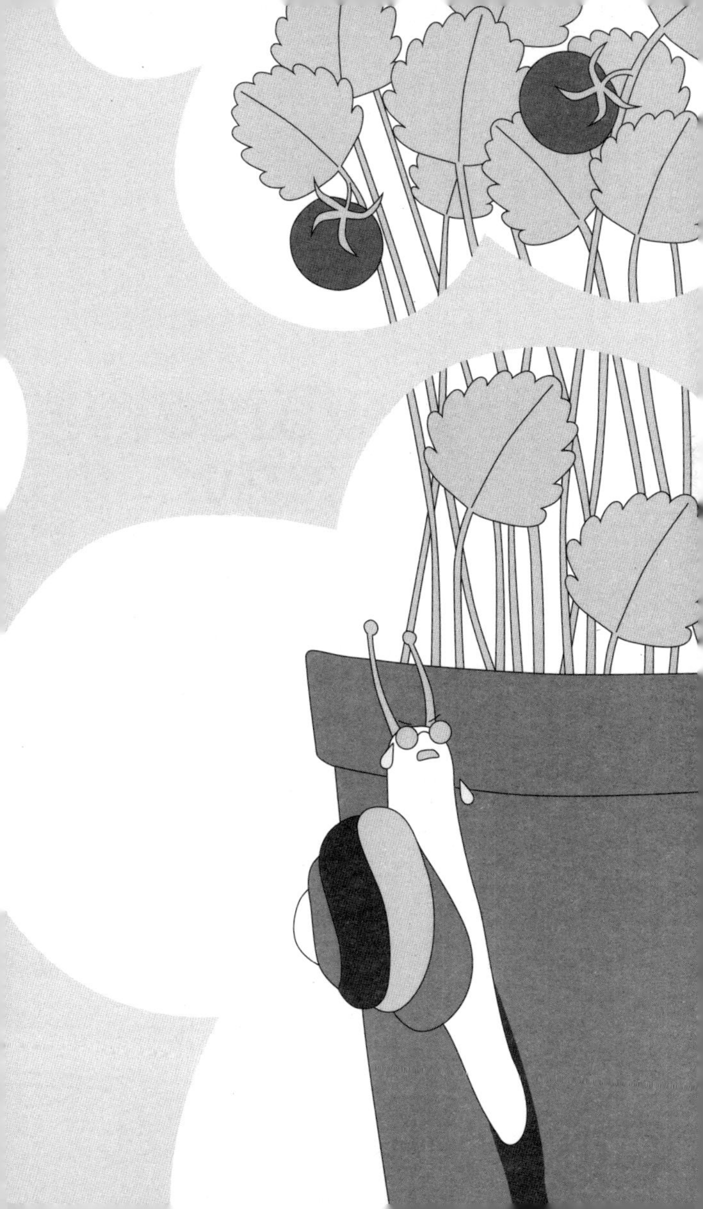

The snail teaches us the magical quality of perseverance and reveals a life full of rewards to come when we learn never to give up, however hopeless we may feel.

There is great wisdom in understanding that hard work does not mean success is guaranteed, but it is still one of life's harder lessons to discover that you can put everything you have into a goal and still fail. The challenge then is to keep going after such a perceived failure and use it as a learning curve. If you do, you'll soon discover that the real key to success is a snail-like perseverance.

72 We all have to learn that falling down is a part of life and that it is the getting back up again that constitutes really living. Falling down is not the end of the journey.

So, when your progress feels slow and the task ahead seems too daunting, keep your snail wits about you and keep going. No matter what.

Top tips to gather your snail wits and keep going to get to your goal!

1.

One small step – or snail slide – away from your dreams. It may be tempting to give up on your goals, dreams and aspirations, especially when you feel you've worked so hard for nothing, but if you quit now, how do you know that things would not have turned around for you with just one more little push?

You may be right on the brink of that success you want, and it may require a little extra step – or snail slide – and you would have now been celebrating that achievement now, or perhaps a different success that came from a perceived failure. If you quit now, you will never know. Perseverance is the hard work you are invited to do when you grow weary of the hard work you have already done. Keep going!

2.

Make room for the magic ingredient: 'time'.

Think of a challenge that you made a success of. This could be a daunting work task or something in your personal life that you had to overcome.

When you think back to how you approached this challenge, did you charge at it like a bull in a china shop? Or did you instinctively slow down, make a detailed assessment of what was needed and then put one foot slowly and surely in front of the other to get the job done? If the answer is the latter, you've already started to be more snail when it comes to challenges that call for patience and perseverance.

Now think about how sometimes we stumble upon the solutions that we are seeking when we just sit back and do nothing except allow time to pass. When this happens, it is almost as if you have an internal 'percolator', which, once you have added the coffee and the hot water, will get on with what it does best and brew a good cup of coffee (solution) for you.

All those who are good at problem solving and working slowly but surely towards their goals will tell you that the secret of their success is to slow down (like a snail) and allow the magic ingredient of time to play its part in reaching a good outcome.

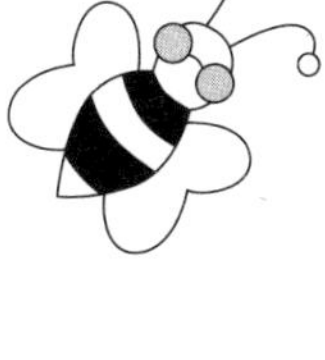

3.

The road is meant to be long. The road to success is long and sometimes perilous, and if you want success that is both meaningful and sustainable, there are no shortcuts. This is because in order to succeed and to feel that you have achieved, you have to reach for your own potential and allow it to unfold in its own time.

Remember, too, that your idea of success will not be the same as the next person's. You are on your own unique path in life and once you become more snail, you will develop the wisdom to know what truly makes you happy and what you need to avoid in order to stay happy.

Just like the snail slowly making its way from A to B, it does not matter how slowly you go or how long the journey takes you. All that matters is that you go safely and do not stop.

Here are some inspiring late-bloomer role models to think about:

✿ Richard Adams wrote his bestselling novel *Watership Down* at the age of 52.

✿ The fashion designer Karl Lagerfield became head designer at Chanel at the age of 82.

✿ The British actress, Dame Judi Dench, worked her whole life in theatre, film and TV but only received all seven of her Oscar nominations after the age of 60.

✿ Toni Morrison wrote her first novel, *The Bluest Eye*, in those moments she could steal between her day job and raising two sons as a single mum. In other words, she relied on her own perseverance to get the job done. She was 39 when the book was published.

4.

Snail dreams. Dream analysts believe that dreaming about a snail or snails indicates the need for patience and perseverance, and that this tiny creature has entered your dreams to remind you that if you stay in the present moment and keep focus, everything will get done.

The core message when a snail appears in dreams is that everything will happen at the precise moment when it should do, so there is no need to rush or panic.

Slow and steady will win the race in your waking life . . .

Snail Fact

Snails are classified as gastropods, a group that includes some 65,000 different species, some of which were around over 500 million years ago. This means the snail has persevered by learning to adapt to thrive in all kinds of habitats and it is this perseverance that has enabled them to survive as a species for so long.

Embrace What Makes You Different

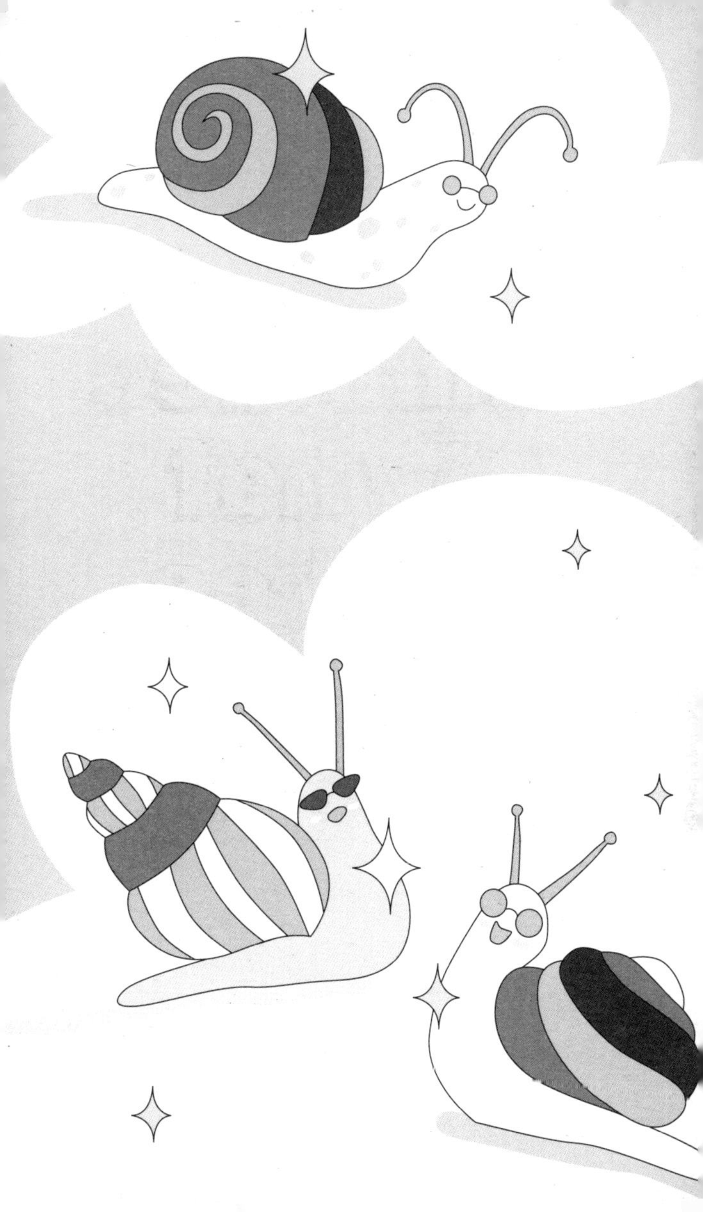

There are 60,000 different snail species in the world and no two snails will be exactly the same. Some live in water, some live on land, and it is this diversity of lifestyle and habitat that explains why, throughout evolution, these mostly little creatures have been so successful.

Even between the same snail species there are small variations – or diversity – in things like their size and even the colour of their shells.

Sometimes the feeling that you are different or 'outside the norm' can be hard to come to terms with, but if you can learn to fully embrace what makes you different you will realise an important life lesson: people who are different are usually the ones who make a difference!

It is ridiculous to expect all humans to conform to 'one-size-fits-all' notions of personality and packaging, and you'd be amazed how many people feel just like you . . . until they learn how they can turn being different to their advantage.

The snail doesn't sit around, hiding under a leaf, thinking why is my shell a duller shade of brown than that of the snail that was chomping through the same cabbage as me? Why am I smaller than a giant whelk? No, the snail is just very grateful to have its protective shell, which allows it to safely blaze a trail to the cabbage patch in search of tasty treats.

When you become more snail, you too will learn how to accept and then embrace those things that make you stand out from the crowd and you will end up feeling fabulously like nobody else, just being you and your own unique and authentic person.

So come out of your shell and embrace your 'difference' and your uniqueness. Here are a few ways to feel pride in being you.

1.

Thinking outside the box leads to success. According to an article called *Being The Odd One Out – Survival Tips To Being Different,* which was published in *Forbes* magazine, all the most successful people simply refuse to conform to society's so-called 'norms'.

These people don't follow the crowd or copy others, instead, they find their own way of doing things, make decisions they know will work for them, set their own goals and go about achieving them in their own unique way.

Even better, they do so unapologetically.

Can you think of a time when you tried to force yourself to think or be like everyone else in the room? Maybe you did that to keep the peace and avoid sticking out like a sore thumb. But if so, what was the little voice in your head saying? The one that won't be silenced no matter how hard you try to fit in. The authentic part of you will not keep quiet every time you try to suppress it, and that's because this is the part of you in charge of making sure you reach your full potential and become the whole human being that you are intended to be.

What would happen if you put that 'voice' in charge for a whole day? Why not try it and see? You will be astonished at how good it makes you feel to be authentic and speak out for what you believe in.

If being kind makes you different, get up on the rooftops and celebrate that difference.

If being fair makes you 'abnormal', take another look at who you are hanging out with and get some better company.

Never forget that being different is what makes you unique, and that in our own lives, just like the snail, we are all different in subtle and not-so-subtle ways, so never try to hide it or apologise for that.

2.

People will love you for the real you, not the fake you. Once you learn to embrace your whole self – including the things that make you feel you are different – you'll start 'vibing' with other authentic people who are different too.

Imagine the changes you can all make in the world once you start celebrating your differences and working together, instead of allowing others to tear you down.

You can also use your 'difference' to teach others compassion and empathy.

Take a moment now to think about what makes you feel different. Is it something to do with your physical appearance? Your personality? Or are you different because of the things you care most about?

Jot down three ways you could use your unique qualities to show other people why it matters (or shouldn't matter) and how they could embrace their own differences too.

It could be that the thing you are hiding is the very thing someone else is desperate to learn and understand more about.

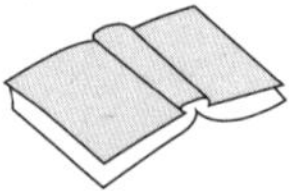

3.

Being different will help you have an impact on the world. The world with all its challenges and discrepancies around social justice, equal opportunities, fairness and wealth distribution doesn't need more of the same to come up with sustainable solutions for our shared issues; what it needs is people who are brave enough to look at things in a new way and suggest solutions to the problems.

Progress is rarely made by staying small and safe or inside your snail shell at all times. Progress is made when you find the courage to be different, step out, use your voice and be counted among those working for the greater good.

You can look to the snail for that courage. If the snail can make a such a noticeable difference to a cabbage patch just by being itself, you can make a big difference in the world by being your true and whole self too.

4.

Live your difference, speak your truths.
Non-binary model and social influencer Rain Dove is a great example of someone who is embracing everything that makes them the unique person they are.

When recently asked about whether beauty standards are diverse enough, they said the problem is less about that and more about why we have beauty standards in the first place.

If you're looking for role models that show us how to embrace being so-called 'different', you'll find Rain Dove at the forefront actively showing the world how to positively embrace and celebrate all our differences.

Snail Fact

The lesser-spotted giant whelk is the world's largest snail. It is an enormous marine gastropod that lives in Australia, where it can grow to a shell length of 70cm. This creature has an unapologetic predatory nature and feeds on tube-dwelling worms. The giant whelk does not ever pretend to be the humble garden snail.

Love Your Small-space Sanctuary

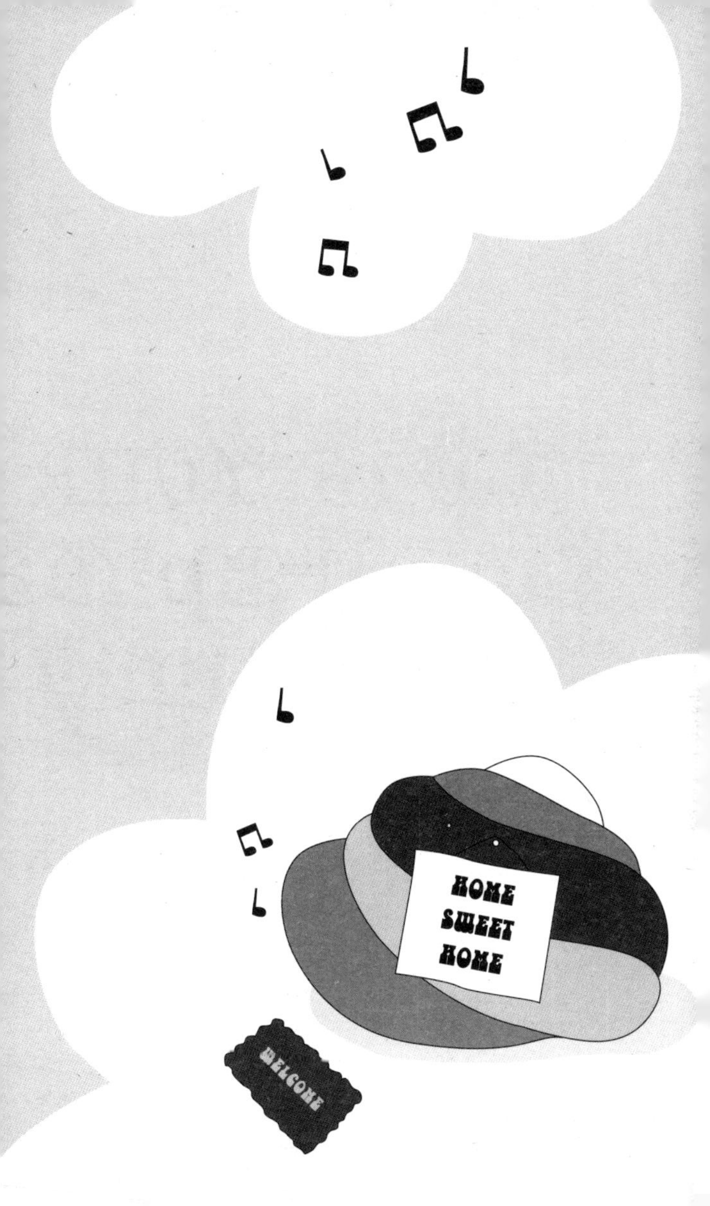
HOME
SWEET
HOME
WELCOME

When it comes to choosing a safe sanctuary that you can call home, the snail teaches us not only that less is more but also that there is an authentic abundance to be found in living with just what we need – no more and no less.

Choosing a smaller living space helps us demand more from the things that we surround ourselves with and the comforts we rely on to create a home that is a sanctuary. For instance, everything you have around you needs to not only look pleasing to the eye, it has to double up as something useful, too. That beautiful vase you picked up at the thrift shop might be perfect for hiding ugly phone cables, and the sofa you sit on might convert into a comfy bed.

And more than all of this, falling in love with a small-space sanctuary teaches us the art of letting go – of all the clutter and things we may be hanging on to but that we don't use or need. Let these items go to new homes where they will be loved, and make space in your modest-sized sanctuary to stretch out at the end of a busy day and bask in the joy of counting your many blessings.

Need help in letting go of stuff to create an uncluttered, small-space sanctuary? Follow these ideas for a simpler life.

1.

Having less means having more. One of the ways that a smaller living space will make you more abundant is that you'll have more disposable cash. Your bills will drop, and you'll realise pretty quickly that there's no point splashing out on things you can't find any space for.

That means you'll have more money to spend on life experiences and expanding your understanding of the world outside your home. Perhaps you'll spend some of this freed-up cash on travelling, or maybe you'll be able to afford to do that self-care course you've always longed to sign up for.

2.

Create a cosy cocoon vibe. If you ask our snail friends they'll tell you that you can't beat the cosy comfort of a small-space sanctuary, and you'll get the added bonus of feeling good about doing your bit for the environment by keeping possessions to a minimum.

You'll notice that the little decorative touches that can get lost in a larger space make a bigger statement when your sanctuary is small. Use accents of colour, and dot around candles and cushions to create the cosy cocoon vibe that only a small space can offer.

Use drawer and shelf organisers to make sure your space stays tidy, because everything has a home, and get into the habit of putting things away so that your space stays uncluttered.

Once you have your small-space sanctuary how you want it, be discriminating about who you invite into your home. If anyone enters with a negative vibe, open the windows to blow out the negative energy and light a candle.

3.

Stronger and lighter. The coiled design of the snail's shell (sanctuary and home) allows the structure to be stronger and lighter, which in turn offers more protection and less onerous mobility. Becoming stronger and lighter are evolutionary advantages for smaller creatures, and you can expect the same benefits when you embrace a smaller home.

You will literally feel lighter because by dragging fewer belongings around with you your energy has become lighter. And you'll feel stronger because you'll no longer have the more burdensome stress and responsibility of financing and running a bigger home.

Feeling lighter and stronger is also an invitation to expand your horizons and engage more confidently with the world. You are pared back, but that means the real and unburdened you can shine through.

Imagine now that you are moving your life into a small sanctuary space.

❁ Aside from essential furnishings, what three luxury items would you take from your existing home with you and why?

❁ What three items do you think you could live without and rehome or give away?

❁ How will you feel when you wake each morning in your new space knowing that your life is clutter-free and hassle-free for perhaps the first time in a long while? Choose one word to describe this new feeling.

❁ How will you celebrate this newfound lightness and freedom?

4.

The quiet life. The snail has downsized for a quiet life and you can do the same.

Like the snail, you can shed any excess baggage and live a simpler life, which leaves you free to connect to what really matters to you.

In a smaller space, you can grow to love the feeling of being enveloped by the silence once you turn off all your gadgets and, like the snail, you will understand this is the safe space that will rejuvenate you for when you need to step into the world.

In your mind's eye, put yourself in this safe, small space.

✿ What can you do to make it a real sanctuary for you to help you rejuvenate?

✿ Do you need music or silence?

✿ Will you light incense or burn essential oils that make you feel more peaceful?

- What kind of soft and tactile fabrics will you choose for cushions and sofa throws that you can sink into when you come home after a busy day in the world?
- How will you fill your cosy home with loving vibes?

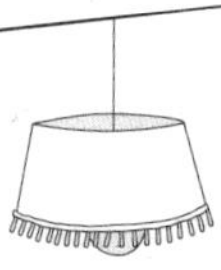

Snail Fact

The world's tiniest snail is said to be so small it – along with nine more of its relatives – would fit through the eye of a single dressmaking needle. The micro-snail species *Angustopila dominikae* stands just 0.86 millimetres small and is so teeny tiny it is nine million times smaller (by volume) than some of the giant African land snails.

Retreat and Embrace Introvert Life

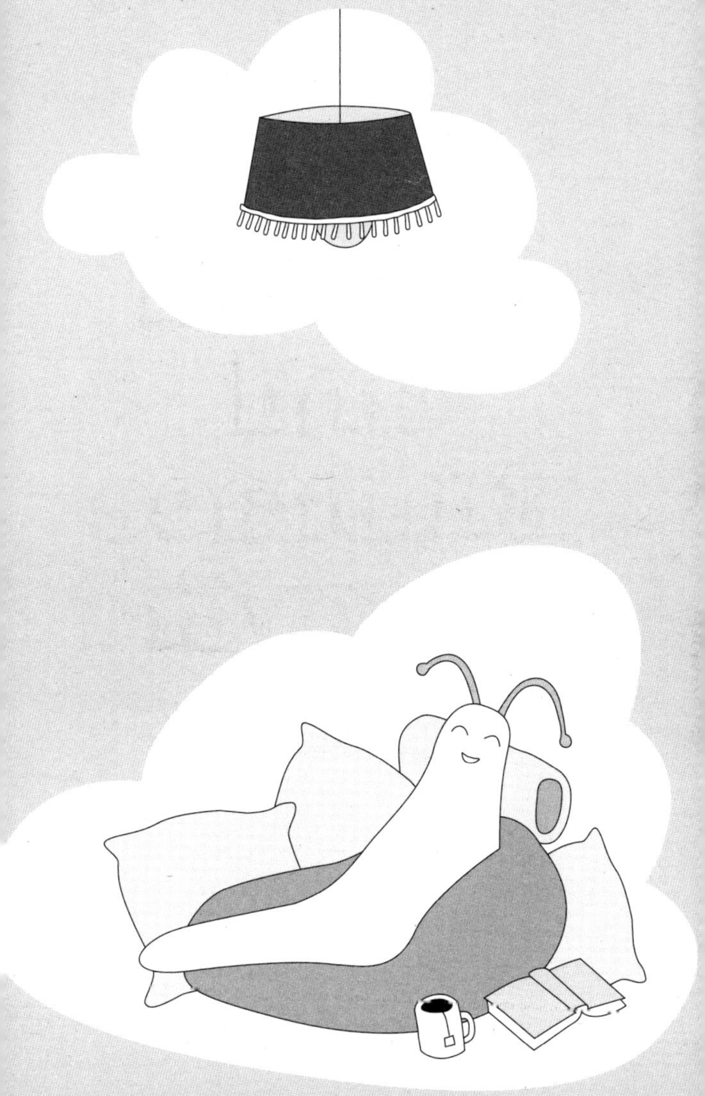

A snail will retreat and sleep when it feels the need to, and in the wild, a snail will protect itself from the cold by hibernating, with some reported to stay dormant for as long as three years!

You probably don't need to go inside and shut the door on the rest of the world for as long as that, but you can learn a valuable lesson from the snail lifestyle guru by accepting there is much to be gained by retreating from the world and embracing time alone every now and then.

Time alone is something that many humans fear, but if you can push through this dread, you will come to learn that when you allow it, the best friend you will ever have is the person looking back at you from the mirror.

When we are constantly surrounded by other people we may be tempted to put our own needs aside and may never even get to know what we are like when we are alone, but when we make an active decision to retreat from the fray and spend some introverted time alone, we discover the real meaning of peace and contentment.

Being introverted does not mean being lonely – being lonely is a state of feeling sad and depressed because you would like more social contact with other people, whereas being introverted simply means you recognise that you need time alone and feel energised by it.

Like our friend the snail, introverts know when to retreat to recharge. They will choose calm over chaos and take all the time they need to get to know themselves, their likes and their dislikes.

Nobody has to be 'on' all the time, and by retreating and allowing yourself to experience the positive qualities of solitude and of being more introvert, you will find more meaning in your life and more clarity about what you want to do with it.

Here are some tips to help you embrace the idea of spending time alone and feel its restorative benefits.

1.

Choosing the quiet life. Snails spent their waking time searching for food, eating, and finding a mate but otherwise, they are pretty solitary creatures. The snail is not afraid of its own company – either in or out of its shell – and you shouldn't worry about spending time alone either.

There are some varieties of snail that like to show off and have boldly coloured, highly visible shells, but the majority favour the quiet life and go about their business camouflaged in shades of white, grey, brown or amber so they can better hide in your garden.

Take a moment to think about the times in your life when you needed to give yourself permission to step away from the limelight.

If you have ever been bereaved, for example, you may have taken an official mourning period before re-joining the world, so you will already know the value of retreat and introspection.

People recovering from illness will also need to retreat from the world in order to heal and regain their equilibrium, and sometimes major life changes like the end of an important relationship or the loss of a job will make you want to do the same.

If you give yourself permission to retreat for a week, how do you think you would spend that time? If your answer is checking social media and WhatsApp messages, you are not yet fully embracing the idea of a retreat as a way of disengaging from what's outside so you can better engage with what's inside.

This takes practice, so don't be hard on yourself if you find it a challenge at first. Build up slowly to being able to comfortably spend time alone and unplugged. Start with a morning, extend that to a day, work up to a weekend and then, when you are more confident about enjoying your own company, try a full week just being on your own.

2.

Looking inwards. Sometimes a snail will retreat so deeply and for so long that it may appear to be dead.

You don't have to go to this extreme, but the more comfortable you become with your own company, the more you will learn to love and respect yourself.

If you want to really know yourself you will have to retreat – just like a snail going back inside its shell – and look inwards.

This is the only way you will really get to know you.

There's nothing selfish about doing this, because if we can truly know ourselves and make the links between our experiences and our behaviours we can become better friends, better lovers, better family members and better work colleagues.

Taking time to reflect on our lives can reveal important information about who we are, what we like, what we want and where we are heading. And just as importantly, it can show us where we may have made mistakes in the past and how we can avoid history repeating itself.

We can even, thanks to time alone, find the courage to face those more difficult thoughts and feelings that we would otherwise want to bury. We then discover that by facing difficult feelings, we grow as people and become more compassionate towards others.

Make a start now by listing three things you like about you. Now list three more!

3.

Trust in you. Just like the snail, you already have everything you need to have a happy and fulfilled life – you have you! The snail trusts its own instincts. It knows when it is time to retreat into its shell and when it is safe to emerge and hunt for food and water.

Listen to your body. It will tell you when you need to slow down, spend some time alone to rest and recharge your batteries.

Listen to your inner voice, too, you will know when it is best to hunker down and lie low and when it is your time to shine and step out and into the full glare of the limelight.

Snail Fact

Snails don't follow any kind of circadian rhythm but they will sleep in bouts of seven sleeps for a stretch as long as 15 hours, then stay awake for the next 30 hours to get their snail jobs done. The sticky mucus they secrete not only holds them safely in one place while they sleep, it also means they can sleep in any position – including sideways or even upside down!

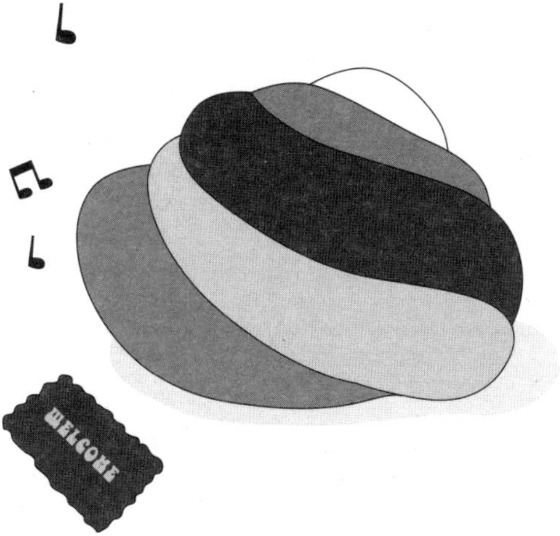
WELCOME

1

Pop Press, an imprint of Ebury Publishing,
20 Vauxhall Bridge Road,
London, SW1V 2SA

Pop Press is part of the Penguin Random House group of companies
whose addresses can be found at global.penguinrandomhouse.com

Penguin
Random House
UK

First published by Pop Press in 2021

www.penguin.co.uk

A CIP catalogue record for this book is available from the British Library

Design: Evi O Studio
Illustrations: Evi O Studio
Text: Susan Clark

ISBN: 9781529149371

Printed and bound in Great Britain by Clays Ltd, Elcograf S.p.A.

The authorised representative in the EEA is Penguin Random House Ireland
Morrison Chambers, 32 Nassau Street, Dublin D02 YH68

Penguin Random House is committed to a sustainable future for our business, our readers and our planet. This book is made from Forest Stewardship Council® certified paper.

FSC
www.fsc.org
MIX
Paper from
responsible sources
FSC® C018179